A COMPENDIUM OF CURIOSITIES™

TIM HOLTZ

ISBN 978-0-615-36424-7

© 2010 Advantus Corp. • 12276 San Jose Blvd. Bldg. 618 • Jacksonville, FL 32223 USA • 904-482-0092 • www.advantus.com

TABLE OF CONTENTS

Our creative surroundings capture the story of what inspires the artistic soul. My studio space is both functional and comfortable to me, it has to be. The elements that adorn it from floor to ceiling are bits and pieces of timeless nostalgia salvaged from findings of the past. Each treasured trinket and fractured remnant fuel my creative passion for all things vintage - each piece of nostalgia has a story to tell. My inks and supplies surround me, displayed on shelves, tucked in bins, but most importantly, within my reach to create at a moments notice. You never know when a creative thought might scurry through the mind so I'm always ready to embrace the opportunity. Transforming those thoughts into "art of the everyday" is my way to incorporate eclectic styles and ideas into the visual chronicles of life.

Date.

Get ready to embark on a journey filled with ideas and inspirations to spark your creative curiosities. This compendium is a compilation of my thoughts and ideas to guide you through your own artistic adventures. I wanted this book to be different though...not your ordinary "how to make" book, but rather "how to create". I believe everyone is truly creative whether they think it or not. It's all about embracing your imperfections and taking time to explore the imaginative. What you'll discover will be wonderful, what you'll discover will be yourself...

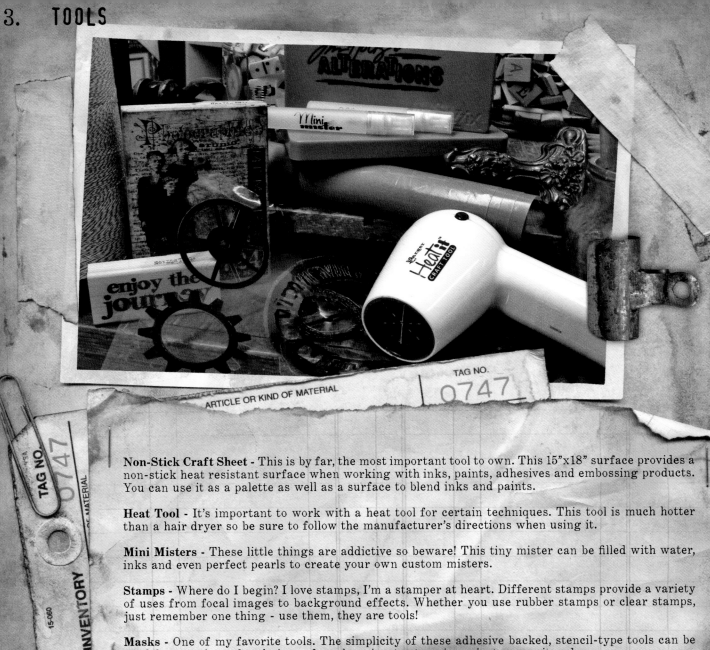

ARTICLE OR KIND OF MATERIAL

TAG NO.

0747

Non-Stick Craft Sheet - This is by far, the most important tool to own. This 15"x18" surface provides a non-stick heat resistant surface when working with inks, paints, adhesives and embossing products. You can use it as a palette as well as a surface to blend inks and paints.

Heat Tool - It's important to work with a heat tool for certain techniques. This tool is much hotter than a hair dryer so be sure to follow the manufacturer's directions when using it.

Mini Misters - These little things are addictive so beware! This tiny mister can be filled with water, inks and even perfect pearls to create your own custom misters.

Stamps - Where do I begin? I love stamps, I'm a stamper at heart. Different stamps provide a variety of uses from focal images to background effects. Whether you use rubber stamps or clear stamps, just remember one thing - use them, they are tools!

Masks - One of my favorite tools. The simplicity of these adhesive backed, stencil-type tools can be used for a variety of techniques from layering to stamping - just you wait and see.

Dies - The ability to cut your own surfaces and embellishments is definitely a great tool to invest in. You can custom cut Grungeboard®, Grungepaper™, cardstocks and even masks.

Tonic® Scissors - Let me just say that not all scissors are created equal. These scissors from Tonic will cut through Grungeboard, Grungepaper, wire, adhesives and much more with ease. Never again will you ask yourself "Which scissor do I need to cut this?" - you'll know.

Paper Distresser - This little gadget is perfect for creating a tattered look along the edges of paper and cardstock. Simply drag the recessed blade back and forth to get the look you want.

Retractable Scratcher - Don't be fooled by this wiry brush, it's a powerful distressing tool. Use it to create scratches in photos and over background by simply swiping it over the surface.

Retractable Craft Pick - This handy pick is perfect for piercing small holes for fasteners, stitching and other odd uses. This pick is tapered so the more you extend it, the larger diameter the pick becomes and best of all it's completely retractable.

Retractable Craft Knife - Sometimes a small blade for detailed cutting is needed and this tool will do the trick. Be sure to work on a cutting mat with this and not your Craft Sheet!

Design Ruler - Sometimes we need to measure, but most often not. Either way this ruler has more than that - a metal cutting edge, a tapered drawing edge and even holes for piercing.

5. TOOLS

Texture Hammer - A small hammer that has four interchangeable tips is definitely a handy tool to have around. This is great for smashing fasteners, texturizing and even the odd fix-it job.

Sanding Grip - Inspired by a trip to the hardware store, this mini version of a standard tool fits perfectly in your hand, has a flat sanding surface and raised sanding edges for detailed areas.

Tiny Attacher - You're probably thinking this is just another stapler? Not really. The staples are the teeniest things ever, plus it goes through thicker stuff like Grunge. Try it - you'll see.

Ink Blending Tool - If you want the ultimate inking tool this would be it. This tool is a wooden handle with Velcro that secures a piece of Ink Blending Foam which is designed to transfer inks from the pad to your surface. It allows you to blend and shade colors unlike anything else.

Distress Inks - Okay, I may seem biased here, but Distress Inks are formulated different than any other dye ink on the market. Whether you're stamping, embossing or distressing, this ink will perform unlike any other ink you've tried before with a palette that's pure distress.

Adirondack® Alcohol Inks - These translucent inks are designed to colorize non-porous surfaces like metals, fragments, gloss cardstock and are applied in a variety of techniques - so get ready.

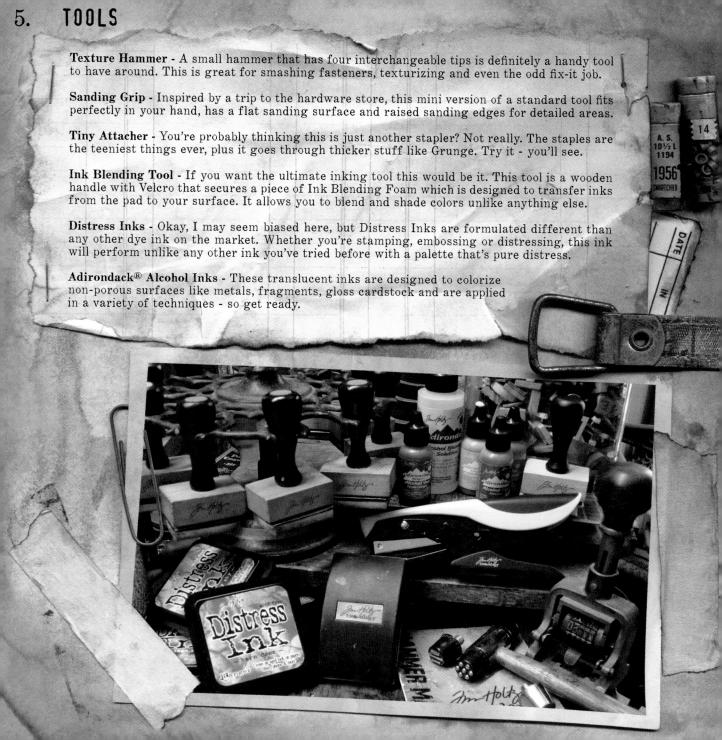

ARTICLE OR KIND OF MATERIAL

TAG NO.
0747

TAG NO. 0747   INVENTORY   15-060   MATERIAL

Adirondack Paint Dabbers - We all need to have a little acrylic paint handy and these dabbers are the most convenient way to paint. Whatever the surface is, these paints will do the job.

Tim Holtz® Distress Crackle Paints - The look of distress in a one-step crackling paint. With the included brush, achieving the look of timeless crackled paint just got a whole lot easier.

Adhesives - Choosing the right adhesive for the type of surface you're working on is the key. Each adhesive has its specialty and recommended surfaces, be sure to choose wisely.

Accents & Bling - Sometimes a project needs a little something extra. Glossy Accents™ is great for a dimensional accent as well as a clear drying adhesive for many things. Looking to add a bit of nostalgic shimmer to your project? Distress Stickles will add the perfect finishing touch.

Perfect Pearls™ - I get asked the most about substitutions for this product and all I can say is there aren't any. This mica powder has a built in binder that does things the other pigment powders simply can't. So if you love the look of luminous pearls - this one is truly "perfect".

Embossing Powders - There are so many types of powders out there. Be sure you have at least the basics - black and clear. Wait until you see what I do with Distress Powders - wow!

Date.

An idea is defined as a concept or thought developed by the mind of what is desirable or ought to be. These thoughts are vital to the creative process and can be simplistic to complex or detailed to quickly sketched. However identified, they should be shared. The next few pages are ideas of random gatherings of my artful thoughts. Give yourself the inventive freedom to try new things and think outside the box. They say art is a chance for your creativity to escape understanding.
— I say let it wander...

ORNATE PLATES:

These ornamental styled bookplates are designed to adorn your most creative projects. Whether it's the scrollwork or embossed bold style, they're sure to complement the look of your next creation...

Accenting the text on a card or scrapbook page is one of the basic uses for Ornate Plates. Simply attach them with coordinating Long Fasteners for a classic finished look. {photo 1}

Another idea to attach the Ornate Plates is using your favorite ribbon. Insert the ribbon through one hole and slide it underneath the plate coming out the opposite hole. {photo 2}

Looking for a way to showcase a photograph? Adhere it in the back of an Ornate Plate and fill the inside with Glossy Accents to create a dimensional raised enameled effect. {photo 3}

Ornate Plates are the perfect base for a variety of jewelry projects too. Add Foliage, Vintage Buttons and Adornments inside to create a wearable piece of art as unique as you. {photo 4}

-1-

-2-

-3-

-4-

FOLIAGE:

Not your typical flowers for sure. These metal elements can be shaped to create a dimensional embellishment of nature's artistry. Foliage can be layered and altered in so many ways to design your own bouquet of creative style...

Use your fingers or pliers to gently bend the petals and leaves to give them a little dimension. Nest and stack them together and don't forget to mix and match the finishes. Secure them with Long Fasteners to create a center. {photo 1}

Foliage on a layout can create both texture and style. Attach them around a photo or title of a page. If the natural metal finish doesn't match your theme, change the appearance using a variety of techniques. {photo 2}

One of my favorite uses for Foliage is jewelry. Combine them with an Ornate Plate and some Link Chain and you have a finished shabby vintage wearable collage. {photo 3}

Canvas is a great surface to attach the Foliage by simply securing them right through the canvas. Combining them with Grungeboard gives the finished project added texture and style. {photo 4}

CORNERS:

I truly believe inspiration is everywhere - especially in things from the past. These corners were inspired by the timeless hardware on old luggage from the journeys of days gone by. The embossed detail and antique finishes enhance a variety of projects...

Right out of the package, the metal Corners can be adhered to anything that has, well... corners! Use your favorite liquid adhesive or strong double sided tape to secure these directly to the corners of your dimensional project like a canvas. {photo 1}

The flexibility of these metal Corners is the perfect solution for giving your photos a finished look. All you have to do is bend the tabs to fold around the back. A few taps from the rubber tip of the Texture Hammer will do the job. {photo 2}

How about using Corners for a mini roof to create a little art dwelling of your own? These fit perfectly on top of Ranger's 1x1 and 1x3 Memory Frames. {photo 3}

My favorite thing about the Corners is their ability to adapt. Whether it's a thin photo or thicker Grungeboard, when you fold over the tabs, they will form to the surface. Here's an idea to finish off your next mini photo book. It's a nice touch don't you think? {photo 4}

-1-

-2-

-3-

-4-

TAGS, TOKENS & STICKS:

It's no secret I love words - these random reminders can make such an impact with their simplicity. The combination of words, letters and numbers of Philosophy Tags, Muse Tokens and Word Sticks tap into my creative soul in so many ways. To attach these elements you have a few options...

The first way to add these is with Long Fasteners. Use them to embellish a book or other altered art project with a collection of your favorite words. Securing them with a Long Fastener allows them to move around a bit instead of being stuck down with adhesive. {photo 1}

Hanging these objects with Ball Chain is another way to attach them when you want to add that dimensional dangle to your next mini book. Simply thread the chain through the hole and secure the chain closed. {photo 2}

Using the words on these findings to help tell your story is one of the best uses I think. I used them on this scrapbook page by hanging them from a Swivel Clasp. To make the words stand out I added some acrylic paint for a customized look. {photo 3}

This cool and funky word bracelet incorporates all of these elements by attaching them with Jump Rings to an assortment of Bead Chain, Ball Chain and Link Chains. I love this idea! {photo 4}

TYPE CHARMS:

The classic look of metal keys with glass overlays capture the nostalgia of timeless correspondence. Create your own custom vintage findings from replicas of these sought after treasures...

Add type charms to cards or ATC's for a customized accent. Attach them with Mini Fasteners or use a Mini Pin to hang them from ribbon. *{photo 1}*

Create unique Type Charms with a variety of possibilities. Using a 1/2" paper punch, punch out scraps of paper to match a layout or stamp a favorite image. Adhere them into the base of the charm with a liquid adhesive, top it with the epoxy sticker and it's finished. *{photo 2}*

Capture vintage photos in a nostalgic way to add to a layout or art project. Mini index prints are perfect for Type Charms or try scaling photos down to fit inside these embellishments. *{photo 3}*

This project can be made as eclectic as your artistic style. Use a variety of included letters, photos or vintage book scraps. Attach them to Link Chain using Jump Rings and you're ready to go. *{photo 4}*

GEARS, SPINNERS & TIMEPIECES:

Time tells a story and each day unfolds a new chapter. Whatever your way of capturing a moment in time is, these elements will provide an industrial look to guide you in the right creative direction. After all, who doesn't like playing games? I think the idea of using these parts together will give any project a hint of interactive interest...

With all of the styles and shapes of Sprocket Gears and assorted sizes of Game Spinners, mixing them all together looks really cool. Stack them up and attach everything together with a Long Fastener to keep everything moving around. {photo 1}

Another function of Sprocket Gears and Game Spinners is to create an entire jewelry piece using them. Each bracelet link is it's own movable gadget. Attach each component together with Jump Rings and you have one steam-punk looking assemblage. {photo 2}

Here's an idea to create a neat compass embellishment. Stack the Gears and Spinners together, secure them with a Long Fastener and hang it as a charm. {photo 3}

Simply capturing a precious moment in time can be achieved using a Timepiece and Game Spinner. This layout shows the birth time of one handsome baby boy! {photo 4}

NUMERALS:

Some find luck in numbers or they have significance for an age or a year in your life. Perhaps they drum up memories of a special day. Whatever the reasons are, numbers can define a moment and let's face it, they have such character...

Add the age to a childhood photograph by attaching Numerals with Long Fasteners. The shiny metal finish was toned down with a little black acrylic paint. {photo 1}

Numerals can capture a date that means so much. Their stylish raised design adds dimension to a card or ATC project. This card combines a variety of textures including grunge, crackle, glitter, ribbon and finished off by a touch of metal. {photo 2}

Collaging over the numbers give them a different look of interest. This Numeral is covered with vintage papers using Multi-Medium. Once a little Distress Ink was added, this was ready to be attached inside a Memory Frame for an artistic pendant. {photo 3}

Altered art is also a great project to use Numerals on if for no reason other than pure randomness. The Long Fasteners can go right through a canvas or use adhesive or beeswax right over the top of them. {photo 4}

-1-

-2-

-3-

-4-

-1-

-2-

-3-

-4-

KEYS & KEYHOLES:

Who holds the key to your world? Unlock your creative secrets and take a peek through these portals of inspiration. Each design of these dimensional elements has the detailing and finishes of classic vintage style...

Add Word Keys and Locket Keys to a book using a variety of chains or a Swivel Clasp. These heavy weight elements add a bit of timelessness to just about anything. {photo 1}

Looking for a way to accent a card or tag. The simplicity of a single word can tell the story. Each Word Key has a single word debossed into it. If it's the key you're after and not the word, just flip it over and the other side is plain. When attaching bulkier objects like these, I like to use wire to do the job. {photo 2}

Create a bit of intrigue by adhering a photograph behind a keyhole. To add a dangling key, insert a Hitch Fastener though the bottom hole and hang it using a couple of Jump Rings. Looks like something right out of grandma's attic. {photo 3}

Of course when it comes to jewelry or wearable elegance, the Locket Keys and Keyholes are the perfect size to create the most adored wearable treasures. Pair them with some vintage beads for a winning combination. {photo 4}

ADORNMENTS & VINTAGE BUTTONS:

Digging through the boxes, drawers and bins of a French marketplace can be very inspiring. The unique findings of these artistic trinkets and ornate buttons will give any project a touch of beauty.

Create a pendant using an Ornate Plate attached to Link Chain with the bird Adornment taking center stage. {photo 1}

This heart has wings that tell a story of love. Whether the style is heart felt or heart of rock & roll, this piece is cool. To color the heart Adornment, use a drop of Alcohol Ink. The wings were cut apart using my Tonic Scissors - yes they cut metal too. {photo 2}

Adding buttons into the center of a flower is nothing special, but adding Vintage Buttons to these collage flowers is. I think these buttons do wonders on anything. {photo 3}

Combine Adornments, an Ornate Plate, a few Vintage Buttons and the Shabby Vintage Papers to create an elegant mini book. I love this idea of using a Vintage Button with a Swivel Clasp to create a closure for the book. {photo 4}

-1-

-2-

-3-

-4-

-1-

gathered
thoughts

-2-

-3-

-4-

TRUST

CURIO KNOBS & FOUNDATIONS:

The ornamental style of vintage cabinetry is the work of a true artisan. What makes them even more spectacular are the intricate findings and hardware that accent them. Dimensional objects like knobs or feet give any project that added detail to finish a masterpiece.

Whether it's precious memories or gathered thoughts a simple Curio Knob onto the front of a mini book or box is just the right element to entice someone to open it up and explore what's inside. {photo 1}

Add the look of vintage beauty to a canvas book with a crystal Curio Knob. Attach it right through the canvas or adhere it to the front. Adding a metal Keyhole, Corners and Foliage give this book a very regal appearance. {photo 2}

This shadow box has the finishing touch of Foundations to create a standing work of art. The ornate design complements just about any theme or style. {photo 3}

However, Foundations don't always have to be used on boxes. Here I used them on a canvas book to give a unique style to a common object. The possibilities are endless with these beauties. {photo 4}

FILM STRIP & RULER RIBBON:

When it comes to details and accents, these ribbons take the cake. Whether it's capturing life's moments on film with the punched projector holes of the Film Strip Ribbon or the nostalgic stitching of the vintage Ruler Ribbon, these elements will give any project the look and texture of days gone by...

The inspiration behind Film Strip Ribbon was the need to always hold film up to the light to see what was in the frame. Why not just add your own pictures? Here I used index photos behind a piece of Film Strip Ribbon on a layout. The smaller photos tell the story to complement my main image. A little adhesive will adhere these right to the back of the ribbon and the transparent windows reveal the rest. {photo 1}

Another cool thing about the Film Strip Ribbon is the little punched holes along each edge. I like to hang an embellishment using a Jump Ring to create an interesting accent. {photo 2}

Ruler Ribbon combines the look and feel of an old canvas tape measure. Just sew right through it to attach it to a card or tag. {photo 3}

Altered projects are the perfect surface for Ruler Ribbon. Weave it in and out of words or images to add interest. {photo 4}

-1-

-2-

-3-

-4-

smiles

FASTENERS & WASHERS:

It's true what they say about good things coming in small packages and it's even better when the things inside are small too. Okay, so fasteners is just a fancy word for a brad and a washer isn't something to put laundry in, but you'll see why these findings are something that are going to be hard to do without...

Whenever I'm trying to secure material or even this rusty mesh, Mini Fasteners work great. I used them to attach this to a canvas for a layered effect. Coordinating them with Long Fasteners for larger objects like the Keyholes gives the overall look a very industrial feel. {photo 1}

Sometimes there is a need to attach smaller embellishments like this mini Game Spinner where the top of a Long Fastener is just too big. Mini Fasteners will go through more layers than you might think. {photo 2}

The rugged construction of a comfortable pair of jeans was the inspiration for this combination. Slip a Long Fastener thorough the slot in a flat Washer and create a faux rivet. {photo 3}

Mini Fasteners have little marks stamped into the tops to look like screw heads. I like to use these as mini hardware elements to accent Grungeboard letters. Be sure to pierce a hole with a Craft Pick first to attach them. {photo 4}

MINI CLIPS & PINS:

Both of these items are considered common objects in the craft world, but their miniature size is not so common. So gather up all of those precious mementos to add to your next project and think of these when glue just won't do...

Attaching an Adage Ticket to a card with a Mini Clip is a great way to create an accent that is movable and removable. These clips are also a great way to secure photos and gift cards inside a card. {photo 1}

Using a Mini Clip to add a charm or in this case a Philosophy Tag to a project is also a fun way to use them. With the addition of a Jump Ring, your element will have the freedom to move around a little. {photo 2}

Don't underestimate the strength of these Mini Pins. I use them to secure all sorts of things to my projects. You can pin them through ribbon to hang your objects, even a Memory Frame. {photo 3}

Adding a Mini Pin to a tag has a definite purpose when paired up with the right image. It's helpful to pierce holes with a Craft Pick first before attempting to stick one of these tiny things through. {photo 4}

TRINKET & MEMO PINS:

Okay, I'll just say it now - these are cute! I don't use that word too often, but seriously? When I look at these, I reminisce about my childhood and having Trinket Pins like this for my locker at the community pool or seeing the Memo Pins at the local butcher shop. Talk about timeless...

Hanging a trinket from a Trinket Pin seems like the most natural thing to do. Actually, they are perfect for securing larger Adornments to a tag or card. Pin them through ribbon or thicker materials like canvas with ease. {photo 1}

One of the best things about the Trinket Pins the tiny words and numbers stamped in them. The Grungeboard heart is accented with the perfect message - a memento of love. {photo 2}

Memo Pins are also great to use a different way, like hanging an Adornment from. Pierce through a project and secure a charm or embellishment through the loop of the pin with a Jump Ring. {photo 3}

This long stemmed Memo Pin has a split ring at the end to secure a tag, photo or this acetate heart. Pin it directly through a card for a unique and dimensional accent. {photo 4}

HITCH FASTENERS:

I think these things look like little trailer hitches don't they? Actually they work about the same way. This two piece embellishment can be used many different ways. Create an 1/8" hole into the base of the project, insert the screw post and then screw on the top of the hitch. Then punch a larger 3/16" hole through the object you want to fasten and cut a slit through it. Slide the large hole over the hitch and presto...

Let's not forget about the hitch design itself. On this layout, I secured a Hitch Fastener onto each corner of a photo and threaded some string around them. Cool huh? {photo 1}

A Hitch Fastener is attached to a Grungebook cover and a Grungeboard hinge is wrapped around and secured over the hitch. Since Grungeboard is flexible, it makes the ultimate book closure. {photo 2}

Another use for Hitch Fasteners is to hang a dimensional object from on a tag or card. Here, a fastener is threaded through the bottom hole of a Keyhole. A Word Key is then attached to the hitch using a couple of Jump Rings. {photo 3}

Creating a jewelry closure is also the perfect way to use a Hitch Fastener. This braided Grunge bracelet utilizes the convenient fastener instead of snaps or other closures. {photo 4}

HINGE CLIPS & D-RINGS:

Attaching a little something here and there on your project not only adds interest, but in this case interaction. Fashioned after larger office type products these clips and d-rings have as much purpose as they do function. Hopefully these few ideas will open up the possibilities for a variety of new uses...

Sometimes I want to hang something off of a mini book but not necessarily on the side with the rings. What to do? How about adding a Hinge Clip and then attaching a Type Charm and Word Key to it? That'll work fine. {photo 1}

Hinge Clips also make a clever way to clip on a card. The hole in the clip fits a Long Fastener so simply secure the fastener through a card and add a photo or other piece of art to the clip. {photo 2}

Believe it or not, Hinge Clips are pretty strong. Strong enough to clip onto a top of a Memory Frame or Fragment to create a wearable work of art. The best part, when it's time to change it out, just unclip it and add another. {photo 3}

I'll be honest, D-Rings make me happy. I'm happy because of their book ring function and straight side which allow my mini books to stack perfectly straight when they're closed. No more bulging books - the nightmare is over. {photo 4}

SWIVEL CLASPS:

A clasp that swivels open with an attached chain that you can hang findings from has unlimited possibilities...

Different sizes of Swivel Clasps give the option of choosing the right one for a project. The included chain is ideal for a book closure. Secure the chain to one end and hook the clasp through the other. {photo 1}

Swivel Clasps can also hang a variety of elements. To open the clasp, just squeeze the wires together and swivel the clasp open. The matching chain comes in handy on projects like this layout where I hung a photo from a ruler. {photo 2}

These clever clasps can also hang from books, canvas and a variety of other art projects. Each end of the chain has a ring to attach something from to create interest. {photo 3}

I use Swivel Clasps the most on jewelry projects. The clasp can hold elements like Locket Keys and the end of the chain adorns a Type Charm. The center of the chain is attached to a piece of Ball Chain with a Jump Ring. {photo 4}

-1-

-2-

-3-

-4-

BALL, BEAD & LINK CHAINS:

Have you ever needed a little piece of chain to hang something? This variety of chain will provide the perfect way to attach elements to any project.

Basic Ball Chain is the most versatile for adding embellishments to a mini book. The best part is this chain can be cut with my Tonic Scissors and in a single package you get over nine feet of chain with eighteen connectors - so cut away. {photo 1}

Bead Chain is a much bulkier form of ball chain. This stuff needs wire cutters to chop apart, but the larger beads have their benefit. Using the small Jump Rings with Bead Chain creates the perfect charm bracelet. The beads are larger than the rings so nothing moves around. {photo 2}

Link Chain has so many possibilities. There are two different sizes of chain in a package along with toggle sets so creating jewelry is a breeze. The simple design of the toggle is great to hang an assemblage of trinkets, beads and treasured findings. {photo 3}

I need to share this because I always end up with scraps of chain and what better way to use them than to twist them up for this funky tangled chain bracelet. {photo 4}

TICKETS & STICKERS:

As a collector of all things lost and found, this collaboration of nostalgic tickets and vintage treasures from my personal collection printed onto cardstock stickers is a simple element to incorporate into a variety of projects.

Oversized and grungy letters are my thing and the Salvage Stickers have a variety of fonts, styles and shapes. The old print block letters look authentic layered inside this frame. Distress the edges using a Sanding Grip and add a touch of Distress Ink for even more depth. {photo 1}

The Salvage Sticker books have so many fun things inside. One of them are these calendar circle stickers sized to fit the Game Spinners perfectly. Coincidence? {photo 2}

The printed words of the Adage Tickets with their antique font capture the moments of the boardwalk. Simple in their design, attaching them to a card or tag with a Tiny Attacher can be just the thing. {photo 3}

Journaling Tickets have a larger surface to be stamped or written on with distressed backgrounds and vintage numbers printed along the edge. I love how these look like they're right out of the ticket booth. Securing them with a Memo Pin adds a dimensional touch. {photo 4}

-1-

-2-

-3-

-4-

PAPER STASH:

They say beauty is in the eye of the beholder. Well, then I can say that these papers are beautiful! Their eclectic style, color palette, elements and all in one design are the ultimate for my paper crafting needs. I hope you'll agree...

Scrapbook pages and larger canvas projects have never looked so good with these designs. Whether your style is the classic film scratches of Retro Grunge, the white wash pastels of Shabby Vintage or the artistic styling of Lost & Found, the double sided cardstock showcases an assortment of design. {photo 1}

Mini books anyone? In addition to the 12"x12" designs, the stash also has the same 6"x6" scaled down designs. No longer do you have to cut apart the best parts of the paper to make a book. A quarter cut of this sheet makes four double sided pages just like that. {photo 2}

ATC or artist trading cards are fun and full of creative expression. Each stash contains coordinating ATC's and borders to match the larger designs. All that's left to do is cut them apart and embellish away. {photo 3}

Snippets are my favorite part of the Paper Stash. This sheet contains 2"x2" double sided versions of the larger 12"x12" so creating matching Fragment Charms and custom embellishments has never been easier. {photo 4}

GRUNGEBOARD & GRUNGEPAPER:

I live for the chance to grunge anything in sight and Grungeboard and Grungepaper is the ideal surface. This paper based product is more pliable, inkable, paintable, embossable and grungable than anything I've ever found...

Grungeboard comes in precut designs as well as basic sheets. This thicker form of grunge can be die cut using your favorite steel die system. For the thinner Grungepaper™, punches and even digital die cutting units can cut through this with ease. {photo 1}

Grunge can also be textured to add a little more interest and help in achieving some pretty cool effects with inks and paints. Use embossing folders to get a variety of textures for your next creation. {photo 2}

The flexibility Grunge offers can be adapted in many different ways. I used them as a hinge on a book or you can create dimensional flowers with Grungepaper by curling the petals. {photo 3}

Sewing through Grunge is an excellent way to not only secure it to a project, but also embellish. One tip I have is to pre-pierce your holes with a Craft Pick and Design Ruler to make hand stitching a bit easier. {photo 4}

-1-

-2-

-3-

IMAGINE
9731

-4-

FRAGMENTS:

The look of something shiny has always caught my eye. Maybe it's the transparent illusions that can be created with it, maybe it's the sheer finish that reflects the light; whatever it is, I'm hooked on using Fragments...

Create custom Fragment tiles using scraps of papers to create embellishments to match your layout. A little Glossy Accents and a good pair of scissors will have you making your next coordinating accents with ease. {photo 1}

If acrylic charms are your thing, Fragment Charms are a must-have. The assorted shapes and sizes in the package allow unlimited possibilities in creating themed charms for your next wearable project. {photo 2}

Another fun way to work with Fragments is incorporating vintage ephemera and your favorite papers to make elements for a card. Here I secured a few Fragment Charms with Long Fasteners as well as glued regular Fragments to the front of the card. {photo 3}

In no time, you'll realize the possibilities of Fragments and no tiny scrap will go unnoticed. Old books, snippets of paper and even transparencies can create unique works of art. {photo 4}

Date.

Learning the manner and ability
with which an artist employs their
technical skill has always intrigued
me. Perhaps it's the inquisitive nature
of childhood mixed with the desire
to play. Whatever the reason, the
explanation of technique is key to
the development of our creative skills.
The better something is understood the
more likely it is attempted. Following
is step by step guidance through my
favored techniques to alter your
creations. Creativity is allowing
yourself to make mistakes
— art is knowing which ones to keep...

33. WRINKLE FREE DISTRESS

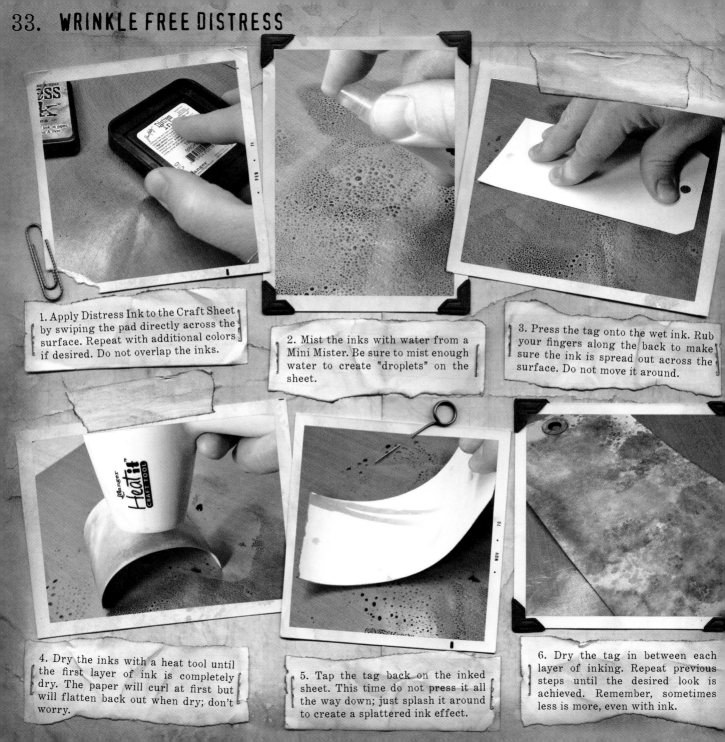

1. Apply Distress Ink to the Craft Sheet by swiping the pad directly across the surface. Repeat with additional colors if desired. Do not overlap the inks.

2. Mist the inks with water from a Mini Mister. Be sure to mist enough water to create "droplets" on the sheet.

3. Press the tag onto the wet ink. Rub your fingers along the back to make sure the ink is spread out across the surface. Do not move it around.

4. Dry the inks with a heat tool until the first layer of ink is completely dry. The paper will curl at first but will flatten back out when dry; don't worry.

5. Tap the tag back on the inked sheet. This time do not press it all the way down; just splash it around to create a splattered ink effect.

6. Dry the tag in between each layer of inking. Repeat previous steps until the desired look is achieved. Remember, sometimes less is more, even with ink.

1. Apply Distress Ink to the Craft Sheet by swiping the pad directly across the surface. Repeat with additional colors if desired - do not overlap the inks.

2. Lightly drag the tip of the glass Distress Re-Inker dropper across the inked sheet. Try different squiggle designs in fast and slow motions.

3. Mist the inks with water from a Mini Mister. Be sure to mist enough water to create "droplets" on the sheet.

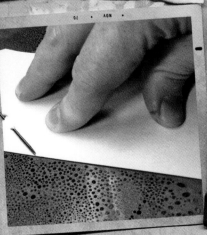

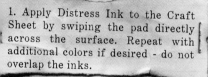

4. Press the tag onto the ink and drag the tag across the sheet. Be sure the entire tag is covered in ink.

5. Mist the tag with water to activate the Distress Re-Inker and allow the ink to spread around and wick out.

6. Dry the inks with a heat tool until they are completely dry.

35. WATER STAMPING

1. Ink the tag with Distress Ink using an Ink Blending Tool by tapping the tool on the ink and working from the Craft Sheet, apply in a circular motion.

2. Continue inking using various colors of Distress Ink until the desired look is achieved. For this technique it's better to ink with bold deep colors.

3. Apply Distress Embossing Ink to the stamp of your choice. This will help the water stick to the stamp image.

4. Mist the stamp with water from a Mini Mister. Be sure you have enough water to cover the image. Sometimes practice makes perfect on this step.

5. Press the stamp onto the inked background and lift off immediately. If you have too much water on your stamp, it's okay, just keep going.

6. Dry the wet image with a heat tool. You'll see your image start to fade as if you've stamped in bleach. Distress Ink is reactive with water.

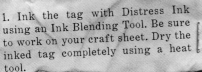

1. Ink the tag with Distress Ink using an Ink Blending Tool. Be sure to work on your craft sheet. Dry the inked tag completely using a heat tool.

2. Stamp an image with Distress Embossing Ink and apply clear embossing powder over it.

3. Heat emboss the image until the powders melt and become shiny and clear.

4. Ink over the entire tag including the embossed design with Distress Ink using the Ink Blending Tool. Notice how the embossing resists the ink?

5. Place a piece of plain newsprint over the tag and iron over it on high heat. This will remelt the embossing powder and absorb it into the newsprint.

6. Continue ironing and slowly remove the newsprint while it's hot. If it cools, it will stick to the tag, simply iron over it again until it lifts off easily.

37. DABBER RESIST

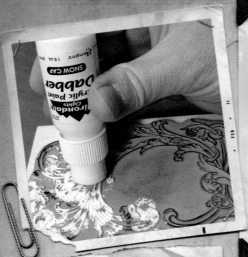

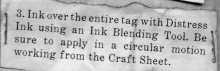

1. Apply paint from a Paint Dabber over a stamp until the design is totally covered with wet paint. I prefer using Snow Cap White for this technique.

2. Press the stamp onto the tag and lift off. Don't press too hard on the stamp or you will smoosh the paint. Add heat to dry.

3. Ink over the entire tag with Distress Ink using an Ink Blending Tool. Be sure to apply in a circular motion working from the Craft Sheet.

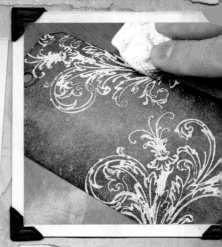

4. Continue inking over the entire tag until you're happy with the colors. Don't worry that you're covering up the paint - that's the idea so far.

5. Mist a cloth or paper towel with water from a Mini Mister. Be sure to use a damp towel and not a baby wipe for this - it will be too wet.

6. Gently swipe over the image with a damp towel to remove the top layer of Distress Ink from the image. The Dabbers resist Distress Ink - cool huh?

1. Create an inked background on a tag using any technique you choose. Dry the background with the heat tool.

2. Stamp an image with a bold color of Distress Ink onto the tag. Note: lighter colors of Distress Ink don't work as well for this technique.

3. Working quickly, apply dry Perfect Pearls powders over the stamped image while the ink is still wet. Work the powders around with the brush.

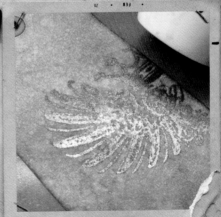

4. Once the image is covered with the Perfect Pearls, remove the excess by dusting them off with the brush.

5. Mist over the tag with water from a Mini Mister. This will set the Perfect Pearls on the tag, but also wick the Distress Ink color from underneath.

6. Allow the Distress Ink to wick as much as desired. Once you like the look, dry the tag with a heat tool to stop the ink from wicking.

39. INKING GRUNGE

1. Tap the Ink Blending Tool on the Distress Ink pad. Be sure to generously ink the tool as Grungeboard is pretty absorbent.

2. Rub the Ink Blending Tool onto the Grungeboard. The surface of Grunge is unique and you need to work the ink into the fibers of the Grunge.

3. Repeat inking with additional colors until the desired look is achieved.

4. Ink the edges of Grunge by using an inked tool and swipe it along the edges. This will create a shadow giving the piece a more worn look.

5. Stamp images with Archival Ink on Grunge. This is a waterproof and a permanent ink which stamps the best on Grunge.

6. If you want to stamp additional images, try working with various colors of inks for a layered effect.

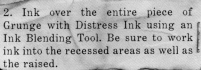

1. Emboss a textured design on Grunge using a Texture Fade embossing folder or other embossing folder of your choice.

2. Ink over the entire piece of Grunge with Distress Ink using an Ink Blending Tool. Be sure to work ink into the recessed areas as well as the raised.

3. Rub a contrasting color of Distress Ink directly over the Grunge hitting all of the raised areas.

4. Rub the darkest color of Distress Ink directly to the Craft Sheet.

5. Swipe the inked textured Grunge face down across the inked sheet to highlight the highest areas for added depth.

6. Ink the edges with Distress Ink using an Ink Blending Tool to create a shadow around the outside.

41. RUSTED ENAMEL

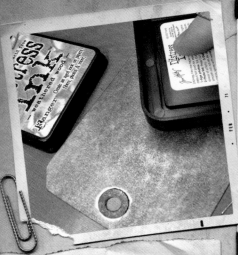

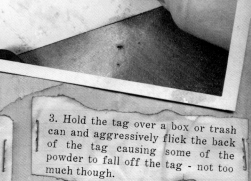

1. Ink the tag by rubbing a color of Distress Ink directly from the pad over the entire surface. Be sure the area is completely covered with ink.

2. Apply clear embossing powder over the whole tag. Since Distress Ink is also an embossing ink, the powder will stick to the entire tag.

3. Hold the tag over a box or trash can and aggressively flick the back of the tag causing some of the powder to fall off the tag - not too much though.

4. Heat emboss the powder until it becomes clear and shiny. Be sure not to over-emboss the image, once it turns clear, stop! Let the tag cool off.

5. Ink over the entire tag with a brown color of Distress Ink using an Ink Blending Tool. Be sure to work the ink into all of the crevices.

6. Wipe off the excess ink from the embossed tag using a cloth or paper towel. If you want to stamp over this, be sure you use permanent ink.

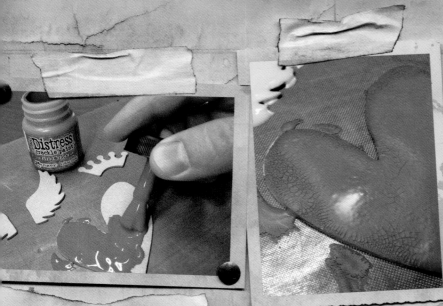

1. Shake the Distress Crackle Paint and apply a medium layer of paint over the surface. Be sure to apply enough paint - think peanut butter or frosting.

2. Allow the paint to start to dry and crack on it's own first. Once it starts to crack, you can finish the process with a heat tool.

3. Once the paint is completely crackled you can ink in the cracks with Distress Ink using an Ink Blending Tool. Be sure to work the ink into the cracks.

4. Mist a cloth or paper towel with water from a Mini Mister and lightly swipe over the inked surface to reveal the paint color, but the ink remains in the cracks.

5. Following the previous steps, apply Clear Rock Candy Distress Crackle Paint over an image and allow it to dry and completely crackle.

6. Ink over the crackled surface and wipe off the excess ink from the crackled surface using a cloth or paper towel to reveal the image.

43. DISTRESS POWDER

1. Stamp an image on a surface with Distress Embossing Ink.

2. Shake Distress Embossing Powder and pour over the stamped image.

3. Remove the excess powder and put it back into the jar. Heat emboss the Distress Embossing Powders.

4. Continue embossing until the color begins to change - dark colors get darker, light colors get lighter. Allow the powders to cool completely.

5. Gently swipe your hand over the cooled powders to remove the "release crystals". These particles never melt and create a timeless embossed look.

6. Ink over the embossed design. The powders will resist any color Distress Ink applied over them. Just wait until you feel the texture!

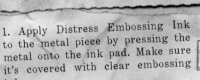

1. Apply Distress Embossing Ink to the metal piece by pressing the metal onto the ink pad. Make sure it's covered with clear embossing ink.

2. Apply Distress Embossing Powder over the metal piece and remove excess powder and replace in the jar.

3. Heat emboss the powders using a heat tool. Remember you're embossing on metal so it's very hot - don't touch it okay?

4. Allow the metal and powders to cool completely before you touch it. This takes longer than you may think!

5. Once cool, begin chipping off the enamel with your fingernail or any gadget or tool you may have lying around.

6. Check out these cool color combinations. I love this look on the metal foliage and numerals.

45. RUSTED GRUNGE

1. Apply Distress Embossing Ink by tapping the pad directly onto the Grunge. Make sure you have enough ink on the surface.

2. Apply Vintage Photo Distress Embossing Powder over the surface and remove any excess powder and replace in the jar.

3. Heat emboss the Grunge until the powders melt and change color tone. The Grunge will curl when it's heated but it's okay, it's flexible remember?

4. Let the powders and Grunge cool completely. Gently rub off the "release crystals" revealing some of the Grunge.

5. Ink over the Grunge with Vintage Photo Distress Ink using an Ink Blending Tool. Be sure to work the ink into the Grunge.

6. Did someone say rust? The color combination of Vintage Photo Distress Embossing Powder and Distress Ink creates the perfect faux rust effect.

1. Ink the surface with Distress Ink using an Ink Blending Tool. Use as many colors as you like.

2. Apply a blob, dab, dollop or squirt of Distress Stickles over the surface. It doesn't matter how, just apply it.

3. Spread the Distress Stickles out with your finger creating a thin layer. These Stickles sparkle more the thinner they are applied.

4. Repeat with additional colors. You can also create your own custom blends by mixing Distress Stickles together on the Craft Sheet - endless combinations.

5. Allow these to dry or heat to dry. Wait a minute - heat? Yes Distress Stickles are a different type of glitter and can be dried with a heat tool.

6. Ink over the glitter with Distress Ink to tint if desired. This will create a more vintage look to your Distress Stickles.

47. ROCK CANDY DISTRESS STICKLES

1. Create a collage on a tag or other surface. Be sure to use a strong paper adhesive for this step.

2. Stamp images using Archival Ink or other permanent, waterproof ink. Make sure your images are dry before moving on.

3. Ink the background with Distress Ink using an Ink Blending Tool to create tinted areas. Remember Rock Candy Stickles are completely clear.

4. Apply a scribble of Rock Candy Distress Stickles over the entire surface.

5. Spread out a thin layer with your finger. Be sure its thin or these will look frosted instead of clear.

6. Allow these to dry completely or dry with a heat tool. They will become very sparkly and clear when dry.

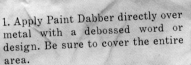

1. Apply Paint Dabber directly over metal with a debossed word or design. Be sure to cover the entire area.

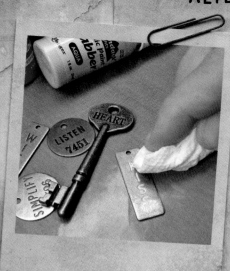

2. While the paint is wet, wipe away the excess with a cloth, paper towel or even your finger. The paint remains in the recessed areas.

3. For metal pieces like Foliage with curves and shape, cover the entire surface with Paint Dabber.

4. While the paint is wet, begin dabbing with a cloth or paper towel to lift the paint off until the desired shabby look is achieved.

5. For detailed embellishments like Ornate Plates, be sure to work the Paint Dabbers into every area. Wipe off excess paint as desired.

6. This technique has endless possibilities in creating coordinating embellishments or giving metal the shabby, vintage, paint washed look.

1. Paint Grunge a base color using a Paint Dabber. Most of the time I just use Pitch Black. Let paint dry.

2. Once paint has dried completely, stamp design with Distress Embossing Ink.

3. Apply Clear Embossing Powder over the image and heat emboss with a heat tool until image is clear and shiny. Allow embossing to cool.

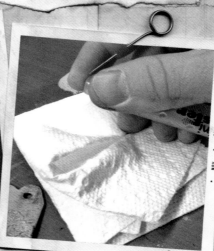

4. Paint over the entire piece of Grunge including the embossed design.

5. Mist a cloth or paper towel with water using a Mini Mister.

6. While paint is still tacky and not completely dry, wipe over the embossed design to remove excess paint leaving behind a shabby wash of color over the design.

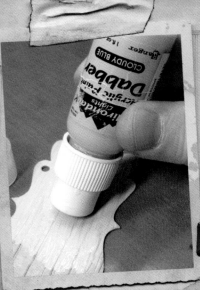

1. Emboss a texture into Grunge using a Texture Fade or other embossing folder.

2. Paint over the entire piece using a Paint Dabber. Blend paint into all of the areas including the recessed parts. Allow paint to dry completely.

3. Sand over the raised texture on the Grunge using a Sanding Grip. The flat base of the sander lets you sand just the high points. Remove the dust.

4. Ink over the entire Grunge piece with a brown color Distress Ink using an Ink Blending Tool.

5. Mist a cloth or paper towel with water using a Mini Mister.

6. Lightly swipe the damp cloth over the Grunge to remove the Distress Ink from the raised areas. The ink has stained any of the sanded and exposed Grunge.

51. ALCOHOL INK MONOPRINT

1. Apply Adirondack Alcohol Ink to the center of a Craft Sheet by dripping or scribbling it around. Use as many colors as you want to.

2. Shake the Metallic Mixative and apply a drop of metallic to the center of the inks.

3. Shake on some Blending Solution over the ink mixture. A few shakes like salt and pepper is enough.

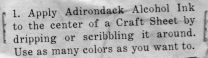

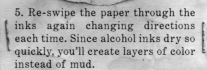

4. Swipe a piece of glossy cardstock gloss side down across the ink mixture on the Craft Sheet. Lift the paper off.

5. Re-swipe the paper through the inks again changing directions each time. Since alcohol inks dry so quickly, you'll create layers of color instead of mud.

6. Stamp images with Archival Ink and dry with heat tool.

1. Drip Adirondack Alcohol Ink onto glossy cardstock.

2. While ink is still wet, hold onto paper with one hand and blast quick, short bursts of air from a can of compressed air to move the ink.

3. Repeat with additional colors being sure to blast each color with air before applying the next. Know when to say when on this - trust me!

4. Apply 3-4 drips of Blending Solution onto the background.

5. Shake Metallic Mixative and add one drop of Mixative into the Blending Solution puddle. Blast this with air too.

6. Once your splattered masterpiece is finished, stamp images with Archival Ink and heat to dry with a heat tool.

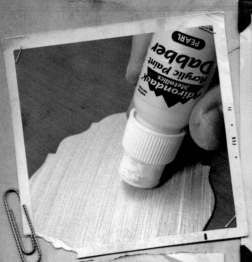

1. Paint the Grunge surface with Pearl Paint Dabber covering it completely and let dry. This can be any surface from fabric to wood.

2. Apply several colors of Adirondack Alcohol Ink onto Ink Applicator Tool. This is the same handle as the Ink Blending Tool, but with felt not foam.

3. Shake the Metallic Mixative and apply a drop of Mixative to the Ink Tool.

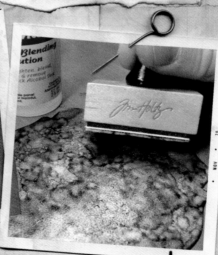

4. Stamp the inked tool over the painted Grunge. Notice how the inks start floating around instead of absorbing into the Grunge?

5. Apply a squeeze of Blending Solution onto the Ink Applicator Tool and stamp onto the inked background. This will blend and move the colors.

6. Once the background is dry, stamp images with Archival Ink and heat to dry with a Heat Tool.

1. Shake the Metallic Mixative and generously apply to the Ink Applicator Tool. Ink over the Grunge surface completely covering it with ink.

2. Scratch over the inked Grunge using a Scratch Tool. Play around with holding the tool in different directions to create more random scratches.

3. Gouge and poke the Grunge using a Craft Pick for an even more distressed and industrial effect.

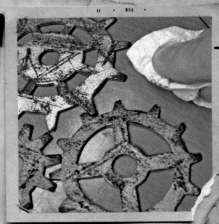

4. Sand and scuff the edges using a Sanding Grip. Be sure to expose the Grunge around the outside.

5. Ink over the Grunge with Distress Ink using an Ink Blending Tool. Work the Ink into the scratches, scuffs and gouges.

6. Wipe off the excess Distress Ink with a cloth or paper towel to reveal a more metallic finish.

1. Apply Adirondack Alcohol Ink to Ink Applicator Tool and stamp ink onto one side of a Fragment. Repeat if needed.

2. Apply Blending Solution to one area of the Ink Applicator Tool.

3. Stamp the Blending Solution into the center of the Fragment to remove the Alcohol Ink. Gently blow to stop the window from spreading.

4. Apply a small amount of Glossy Accents around the edge of the inked side of the Fragment.

5. Place Fragment over a photograph or stamped image.

6. Trim off excess paper with Non-Stick Scissors right up to the edge of the Fragment. Your image is revealed through the tinted Fragment.

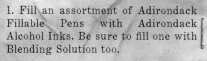

1. Fill an assortment of Adirondack Fillable Pens with Adirondack Alcohol Inks. Be sure to fill one with Blending Solution too.

2. Use the pens to colorize smaller metal embellishments. To build color intensity, simply add layers of ink.

3. Also colorize metal hardware including Tiny Attacher Refills, Eyelets and Long Fasteners. Match your projects perfectly.

4. For larger embellishments, apply Alcohol Inks using the Ink Applicator Tool.

5. To create the most vibrant color on elements with lots of detail, simply drip the Alcohol Ink directly on the object. Heat to dry with a Heat Tool.

6. There are so many possibilities to colorize any non-porous accent or embellishment. Start inking!

57. COLORFUL LAYERED FRAGMENTS

1. Stamp an image onto one side of a Fragment with Archival Ink and let dry. If heat setting, be careful as Fragments can melt if too hot.

2. Place the Fragment stamped side down onto white paper and begin coloring on the back with the Adirondack Fillable Pen filled with Alcohol Ink.

3. Continue coloring and blending colors using a variety of filled pens. The Alcohol Inks blend colors with ease on slick surfaces.

4. To remove any of the colors, use a pen filled with Blending Solution. Works as a great eraser or if you want to lighten any areas.

5. Apply a small amount of Glossy Accents around the outside edge of the inked side of the Fragment.

6. Adhere to a piece of white glossy cardstock and trim off excess with Non-Stick Scissors.

1. A Mask is a stencil-type tool made from adhesive backed vinyl. These are available either predesigned or blank to design your own.

2. Before you begin working with Masks it's important you follow the prepping directions to remove any of the excess cut-outs from your design.

3. You can also create custom masks from Blank Mask Sheets using your personal die cutting system.

4. For smaller Masks you can also create them from Blank Mask Sheets with a variety of punches.

5. Make a custom Mask for that stamp you always use. Just stamp the image with Staz-On ink on the Blank Mask Sheet and cut it out.

6. With the proper care and storage, Masks can last quite a while. Wash with soap and water and store them on the included clear storage sheets.

59. INKING AND STAMPING MASKS

1. Create a background on a tag and stamp the image. Make sure all of the inks are completely dry.

2. Place custom Mask over the stamped image. Because the Mask is clear, lining everything up perfect is simple.

3. Ink over the tag with Distress Ink using an Ink Blending Tool. You'll see exactly how the finished tag will look since the Mask is clear.

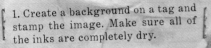

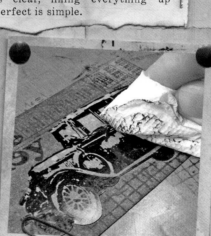

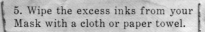

4. Stamp over the masked tag with a water-based dye ink or Archival Ink.

5. Wipe the excess inks from your Mask with a cloth or paper towel.

6. Carefully and gently lift off the Mask from your tag. Your image was completely protected and floats over all of your coloring and additional images.

1. Create custom pearl "mist-ure" by adding one full dropper of Distress Re-Inker into an empty Mini Mister.

2. Add one scoop of Perfect Pearls pigment powders into the mister. You can use anything for a scoop, I use a craft stick since it fits.

3. Fill the Mini Mister with water and shake well to emulsify the contents. Be sure to do this step to avoid your mixture separating later.

4. Place Mask onto your surface and burnish it well to make sure it is stuck to the surface.

5. Mist over the Masked area with custom mist. One helpful tip is to blot the excess ink from the Mask to avoid the ink seeping underneath.

6. Gently and carefully remove the Mask to reveal your design. If the paper is still damp you can dry it with a Heat Tool once the Mask is removed.

61. EXTREME MASKING

1. Place Mask on tag and Ink with Distress Ink using an Ink Blending Tool. Be sure to use bold colors for this step.

2. Gently remove the Masks and mist the entire background with water from Mini Mister until Distress Inks start to wick and move around.

3. Dry the tag using a Heat Tool.

4. Reposition the Masks and stamp over the tag using a variety of images. Wipe the excess ink from the Masks and gently remove them.

5. If you created a custom Mask, cut out an area around your cut design so you have a negative Mask. Place this over the main design and stamp inside.

6. Wipe off any excess ink from the Mask and gently remove it to reveal your finished layered masterpiece.

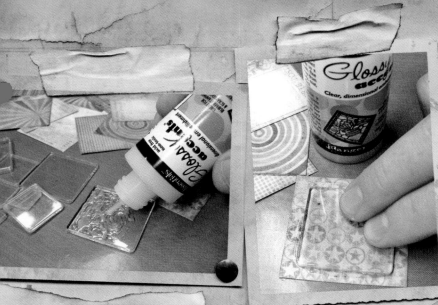

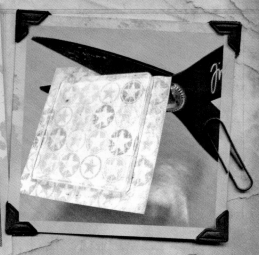

1. Apply Glossy Accents to one side of a Fragment. Use the tip of the bottle to move it around. Glossy Accents works as a great clear drying adhesive.

2. Place adhesive side down over paper and move in a slight circular motion to spread out the accents. Press down on the Fragment to remove air bubbles.

3. Trim off the excess paper with Non-Stick Scissors. Trim as close to the edge of the Fragment as possible.

4. Apply Glossy Accents to one side of a Fragment. Use the tip of the bottle to move it around.

5. Press the Fragment adhesive side down onto a transparency. Allow the Fragment to dry completely before cutting out with a Craft Knife.

6. Use these pieces to embellish a variety of your projects. Use the transparent Fragments over words or journaling on your projects too.

63. DIMENSIONAL COLLAGE FRAGMENTS

1. Place a Fragment onto vintage paper and trace around the outside. You must use thin vintage paper for this technique to work the best.

2. Position and adhere flat elements within the sized area using Glossy Accents. Anything outside of your outline will be cut off later.

3. Apply Glossy Accents to one side of a Fragment. Use the tip of the bottle to move it around. Glossy Accents works as a great clear adhesive.

4. Press the Fragment onto the background lining it up with the outline.

5. Flip the entire Fragment and paper over and press the paper onto the back into the recessed areas of the collage.

6. Trim off any excess paper with Non-Stick Scissors. Be sure to trim as close to the edge of the Fragment as possible.

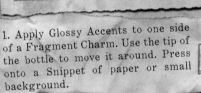

1. Apply Glossy Accents to one side of a Fragment Charm. Use the tip of the bottle to move it around. Press onto a Snippet of paper or small background.

2. Flip the entire piece over and apply a strip of clear packing tape over the back of the paper. This is will give the back of the charm a protective film.

3. Trim any excess tape and paper from around the Fragment using Non-Stick Scissors. Do your best cutting around the top of the Fragment Charm.

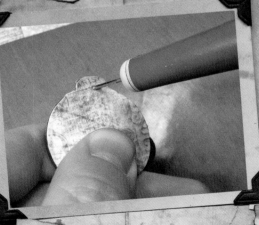

4. Using a Sanding Grip, sand off any excess paper around the top of the Fragment Charm and smooth any rough paper edges.

5. Pierce a hole with a Craft Pick through the paper working from the back of the Fragment to the front.

6. Create coordinating Fragment Charms for cards and scrapbook pages using Snippets or scraps of matching papers.

65. GRUNGEPAPER FLOWERS

1. Alter a piece of Grungepaper using a technique of choice. Here I glued vintage papers to a piece and die cut an assortment of flower shapes.

2. To curl the petals, working from the back of the flower, pinch the end with your fingers as shown.

3. Place the flower on a flat surface and continue rolling each petal into the center of the flower.

4. Repeat for all of the flower petals as shown. You can curl the petals as tight as you want.

5. Create a variety of looks by curling the petals in different directions.

6. Ink the edges with Distress Ink using an Ink Blending Tool and layer the flowers by stacking together. Embellish with buttons or charms.

1. Apply Matte Multi-Medium to a piece of vintage paper. Make sure to apply a generous layer of medium.

2. Press a Numeral or other object you want to cover face down into the wet Multi-Medium.

3. Flip entire piece over and press the paper around the object forming the paper to it's shape. Set aside to dry.

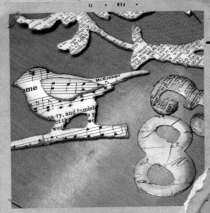

4. Carefully tear off the excess paper around the object.

5. Using a sanding grip, smooth the excess paper off of the edges of the element to create a finished look.

6. Try this technique to cover various objects including metals, Grunge, canvas, book covers and anything else you're getting tired of looking at.

67. DESIGN DETAILS

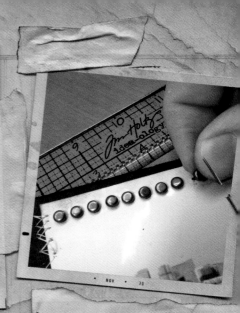

1. Place a Design Ruler along the edge of the surface. Use the grid to line up where you want the holes.

2. Using a Craft Pick, pierce through the Design Ruler. The holes are spaced evenly so you can decide how far apart you want them.

3. Insert Long Fasteners through the holes and secure them in the back. Repeat for all of the holes.

4. Place the surface onto the Hammer Mat and tap the tops of all of the Long Fasteners with the "bumpy" tip of the Texture Hammer to dent them up.

5. Place the grid lines of the Design Ruler along the edge of the surface placing the holes along the edge. Pierce two sets of holes side by side.

6. Stitch through the holes with wire or thread to create a hand-stitched effect.

Date.

Inspiration is all around us, just learn to pause...or nothing worthwhile will catch up to you. The ideas and techniques in this book were a way to convey my creative thoughts. Hopefully you found a sense of artistic motivation scattered through the pages of these works. In the words of Albert Einstein: "Imagination is more important than knowledge. For while knowledge defines all we know and understand, imagination leads us to all we might yet discover and create."

— so remember to enjoy the journey.

69.

71.

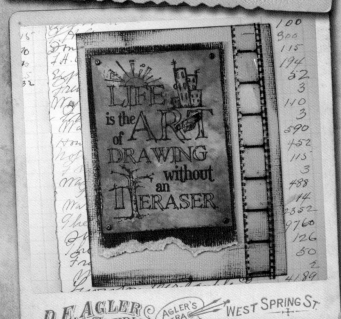

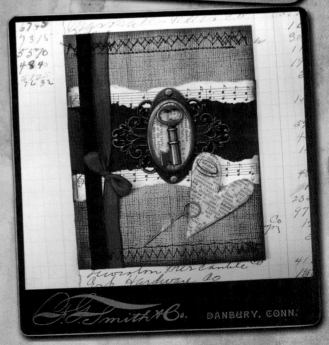

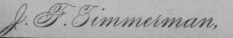

73.

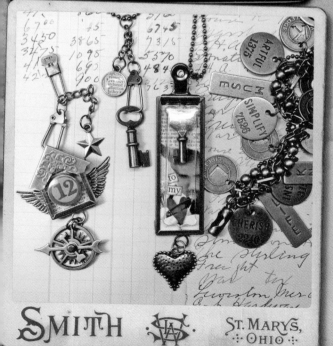

creativity is allowing yourself to make mistakes. art is knowing which ones to keep.

SOAR

SMITH · ST. MARYS, OHIO

G. G. Shellabarger, KANSAS.

DANBURY, CONN.

74.

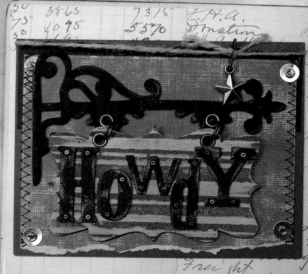

MEMORANDA.

Date.

Notes to Self—

Advantus Corp. – The Tim Holtz® idea-ology™ line – Tools: Design Ruler, Texture Hammer, Sanding Grip, Tiny Attacher, Tiny Attacher Refills, Mask; **Embellishments:** Ornate Plates, Foliage, Corners, Philosophy Tags, Muse Tokens, Word Sticks, Type Charms, Sprocket Gears, Game Spinners, Timepieces, Numerals, Word Keys, Keyholes, Locket Keys, Adornments, Vintage Buttons, Curio Knobs, Foundations, Film Strip Ribbon, Ruler Ribbon, Fragments; **Fasteners:** Long Fasteners, Washers, Mini Fasteners, Mini Clips, Mini Pins, Trinket Pins, Memo Pins, Hitch Fasteners, Hinge Clips, D-Rings, Swivel Clasps, Jump Rings, Ball Chain, Bead Chain, Link Chain; **Paper:** Paper Stash – Retro Grunge, Shabby Vintage and Lost & Found; Adage Tickets, Journaling Tickets, Salvage Stickers, **Grunge** - Grungeboard®, Grungepaper™ {*Advantus Corp.* • www.timholtz.com}

Ranger Industries – Inks: Tim Holtz® Distress Inks, Tim Holtz Distress Clear Embossing Ink, Adirondack® Alcohol Inks, Adirondack Alcohol Ink Metallic Mixatives, Adirondack Blending Solution, Archival Ink™; **Paints:** Tim Holtz Distress Crackle Paint; Adirondack Paint Dabbers; **Tools:** Non-Stick Craft Sheet™, Heat-It™ Craft Tool, Adirondack Alcohol Ink Fillable Pens, Mini Mister, Ink Blending Tool, Ink Applicator Tool; **Other:** Tim Holtz Distress Stickles™, Tim Holtz Distress Embossing Powders, Glossy Accents™, Perfect Pearls™, Claudine Hellmuth Studio Matte Multi-Medium, Claudine Hellmuth Sticky-Back Canvas, Memory Frames, Memory Glass and Memory Capsules. {*Ranger Industries* • www.rangerink.com}

Stamper's Anonymous – Tim Holtz collection of Rubber Stamps {*Stamper's Anonymous* • www.stampersanonymous.com}

Sizzix – Tim Holtz Alterations collection of dies and texture fades {*Sizzix* • www.sizzix.com}

Tonic® Studios – Tim Holtz Scissors, Paper Distresser, Retractable Craft Pick, Retractable Craft Scratcher, Retractable Craft Knife {*Tonic Studios* • www.tonic-studios.com/timholtz}